54 Secrets
To Playing Better Golf™

By
"Robert George" Markovics

Jean Berg
Editor

Copyright © 2009 by Robert George Markovics

All rights reserved. No portion of this book may be reproduced, stored in a retrieval system, or transmitted in any form or by any means - electronic, mechanical, photocopying, recording, scanning, including the right of reproduction in whole or part in any form, except for brief quotations in critical reviews or articles, without the prior written permission of the author. For information, contact the author.

The information in this book is distributed without warranty. Although every precaution has been taken in the preparation of this book, neither the author nor printer shall have liability with respect to any loss or damage caused in any manner by the information contained in this book.

54 Secrets to Playing Better Golf may be purchased in bulk at a discount for educational, business, fund-raising, or sales promotional use. For information, please email the author at rgm@golf54secrets.com.

This book has been self published with help and guidance from Friend Printing 600 Dairy Street in Monett, MO 65708. Editing was provided by Jean Berg, Executive Director of the Barry-Lawrence Regional Library in Monett, MO. The cover design was provided by Matt Willis of Friend Printing. The Web page was developed by Stacey Willis-Center of Aurora, MO.

ISBN 10 – 0615355811
ISBN 13 – 978-0-6153558-1-8

Copyright – Txu001657090

Printed in United States of America

Preface

Golf is a humbling game. It has a way of weakening the strong, outwitting the intelligent, rewarding poor performance, presents luck at the most unusual time, turns its back on perfection; and most of all, it brings us back time and time again to try and conquer the course and us. The search for the perfect swing is an endless endeavor. I believe the perfect swing resides with the golf gods. We mortals are to enjoy the game and each other, while the perfect swing sits on a pedestal in some far away secret location.

Few golfers have known the elated feeling of shooting par. An even lesser number of players ever have the feeling of walking off the 18th green knowing they tamed a course.

Even though I have been sub par many times in my career, my greatest joy in golf has been meeting people who are complete strangers. Golf has permitted me to enjoy being outdoors, opened doors when least expected, given me the chance to explore other lands, learn about other cultures, and most of all it has taught me lessons that have been valuable in life.

Oddly enough, golf has been my private sanctuary when times got hard. It was the one place I could go and be alone to work through a problem or search for answers to questions. It has helped me find my way at times. Golf is a journey that can be taken with others or quietly alone. Either way, the journey is worth the trip. I am thankful I have experienced the journey both ways in my life.

I hope this book will allow golfers all over the world to use a simple process designed to help them lower their score and find greater enjoyment playing golf. If it does, then golf has again helped me cross another bridge to possibly meet more people in faraway lands. Maybe we will have the chance to play someday.

Purpose of the Book

For many years, I have been fortunate to play golf all over the United States, and I have met people from all around the world. Meeting people from other cultures has been rewarding and educational. There were times when the language barriers prevented a lot of communication. However, good golf shots seem to neutralize the speaking void when your playing partner grins and nods with approval at your shot.

Golf has enabled me to transcend political and religious differences. It introduced me to the fact that golfers everywhere have a great appreciation and respect for fellow players who pull off the impossible shot, make a long putt, or hit a shot that produces the sound of a well struck ball. There is a bond between players at this defining moment.

One day, it occurred to me that most golfers rarely have the opportunity to enjoy golf. They toil endlessly searching for a swing. As a result, I began to re-examine my own game to see if I could develop a process that would help other players enjoy golf each and every time they played.

In January 2003, when it was about twenty degrees outside, I donned my favorite long sleeve red Razorback turtleneck shirt, put on some corduroy pants, thick wool socks, and of course my golf shoes. Stepping off thirty paces, I began pitching the ball towards a bucket. Granted, I only lasted for twenty-five shots, but I was committed to finding a way to help golfers everywhere experience greater enjoyment playing a game they love.

Over the next four years, I continued searching for a process that would help the weekend golfer score in the low eighties on a regular basis. So that became the purpose of this book, **"Develop a process to help golfers around the world lower their scores and find greater enjoyment playing golf"**☺!

Table of Contents

A.	Focusing on Fundamentals	Pg	1
B.	The Best Place to Start is Learning to Putt	Pg	8
C.	Chipping	Pg	13
D.	Pitching, Fairway Shots & the Tee Ball	Pg	16
E.	Club Selection	Pg	20
F.	Course Management or Strategy	Pg	23
G.	Managing Predicaments	Pg	27
H.	Playing from the Sand	Pg	30
I.	The Mental Side of Golf	Pg	36
J.	Course Etiquette	Pg	38
K.	Tracking Your Performance	Pg	40
L.	Golf Terminology	Pg	41

Author's Note – 54 Secrets has been written from the perspective of a right-handed golfer.

A. Focusing on Fundamentals

I have a strong belief that regardless of what you do in life, fundamentals are needed to achieve excellence. In golf, there are six basic fundamentals required to build a successful golf game. Let's review the six fundamentals that have enabled me to have greater consistency and more enjoyment playing golf.

The 1st Fundamental – Grip
Regardless of whether the player is an amateur or professional, female or male, young or old; all golf swings must incorporate a good grip on the club.

Secret # 1 - The grip allows the body and club to become one instrument☺.

We have eight fingers and two thumbs on our hands. However, we use just five fingers to hold the club. These five fingers are the pinky, ring, and middle finger of the left hand and the middle and ring finger of the right hand. The other fingers and thumbs rest gently on the club. When the left hand is positioned on the club, one should see two knuckles of the left hand (the index and middle finger). The right hand thumb is placed left of center line creating a "V" shape down the shaft.

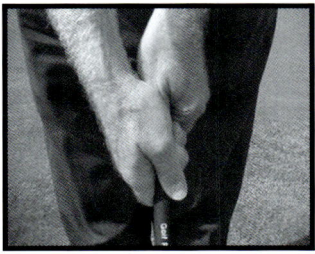

The pinky finger of the right hand has two options. One, is for the pinky finger to interlock between the index finger and the middle finger of the left hand. Two, is for the pinky finger to overlap between the index finger and the middle finger of the left hand.

Overlapping Grip **Interlocking Grip**

Secret # 2 – Use the interlocking grip to putt and the overlapping grip for everything else☺.

The 2nd Fundamental - Hand Position at Address

Hand position, when setting up for a shot, is critical to get proper release at impact. When observing most players, I notice two prevailing errors in their initial set up:

* Forward pressing the hands in front of the ball
* Drooping hands behind the ball

Both of these hand positions make it impossible for the golfer to square the club face at impact. Thus, golfers sacrifice maximum distance and backspin on the shot. The end result produces a shot that is not rewarding or stimulating. The hand position I have found to produce the best results is where the hands are slightly ahead of the ball at address.

Secret # 3 - When a player starts the backswing with his/her hands, good impact between the club face and ball is highly improbable. Starting a backswing from the shoulder produces the best results☺.

The 3rd Fundamental – Stance

There are many different stances one may utilize to address the golf ball. However, the objective is to find one address position (stance) that helps generate solid impact and consistency. There are two observations I have noticed regarding a player's stance:

* A narrow stance produces a forward weight shift (on the toes) during the down swing. The reason is because the body's center of gravity is higher up the spine towards the shoulder blades. Thus, good impact is improbable.

Secret # 4 - When the outer edge of your shoes is inside the width of the shoulders, your stance is too narrow☺!

* Too wide a stance prohibits the player from starting the golf swing from the shoulder. Thus, once again, good impact becomes highly improbable.

Secret # 5 - When the instep of your feet is outside the shoulders, the stance is too wide☺!

I have found the best set-up is when you draw a line from the edge of the shoulders to the center line of the shoes (toe to heel). This allows one to achieve the best center of gravity to produce a compact and consistent swing.

Secret # 6 - The center of gravity on the spine needs to be between the hips and the bottom of the rib cage☺.

For me, once I take a stance, I have discovered that moving my right foot about two (2) inches farther right lowers my center of gravity down the spine. This allows for a compact swing, greater consistency and more power at impact.

The 4th Fundamental – Ball Position
My focus is to play each shot from the same ball position regardless of club selection. This approach helps me keep the game simple and consistent. I find it easier to adjust the club selection process rather than have several different swing patterns. After a lot of experimenting; the best ball position was off my left heel. This spot is where my swing generally bottoms out. This optimum ball

location may vary between players depending on height and weight.

Secret # 7 - Finding the optimum ball position between the feet improves the opportunity to achieve good impact. Maximum impact generates more back spin and greater distance☺.

The following process will help you find the best ball position to achieve better impact.

1) Keep your feet together with the ball in the middle. Hit twenty balls to a target 40 yards away.

2) Slowly widen the stance approximately six inches at a time keeping the ball in the center of your feet. Remain focused on hitting twenty balls to a target 40 yards away.

3) Widen the stance again, another six inches at a time. Keep the ball in the center of your feet. The ball should begin landing to the right of the target.

4) When you're comfortable with a wider stance, move the ball towards the left foot approximately two inches at a time. You will begin to feel a different impact the farther left you move the ball.

5) As you approach the point where the swing bottoms out, two events will occur:

* The balls will begin grouping on target
* You'll begin to feel the club face meet the ball

When this happens you will have found the best ball position in your stance. Now you are beginning to experience the sweet spot, a.k.a. – impact.

54 Secrets To Playing Better Golf

Secret # 8 - If you use the same ball position for all shots, your game is easier to manage and performance is greatly improved☺.

The 5th Fundamental – Balance
Balance during the golf swing is highly critical. If a player loses his/her balance in the backswing, squaring the club face at impact is lost. To develop greater consistency, I make sure to apply slight pressure on my heels. This is similar to a baseball player standing in the batter's box. Pressure on your heels allows you to keep the lower body and upper body in tune with each other. In addition, this small adjustment helps keep the swing smooth, and I have found my back swing is reduced to a ¾ swing, improving consistency and accuracy.

Secret # 9 - If you produce a ¾ swing and square the club face, you gain more distance because you generate more power with less effort. Thus, better impact is achieved☺.

The 6th Fundamental – Aiming the Club Face
Aiming the club face at a target takes practice. If you lack discipline to aim the club face, you can be assured the ball will find the wilderness. To help me through the process, I first stand behind the ball and visualize the ball's imaginary flight line to the target.

Then I look for a mark in front of the ball on the ground. I aim the club face at the mark using this spot as my guide to the flight line. Now I'm set to follow my pre-shot routine to create the best possible swing to impact the ball.

Packaging the Fundamentals into a Pre-shot Routine
Now that we have reviewed six fundamentals to utilize; let's package them into a pre-shot routine (order) that helps us achieve a consistent swing at all times.

1) Position the hands on the club and set the grip
2) Aim the club face (positioning the club face behind the ball)
3) Take your stance (keep feet together, ball in the middle)

4) Begin widening your feet and position the ball in the stance
5) Establish your hand position slightly ahead of the ball
6) Finalize your balance

This approach follows a logical course of action starting at the point where the club and ball meet. Now you have established a process that should help you play consistent golf. In short, your starting point is the ending point (where the club face and ball meet) when you prepare to make a shot.

Secret # 10 - A consistent process helps you achieve the best possible impact on each shot. Thus, you have the greatest opportunity to achieve a greater level of performance and enjoyment☺.

B. The Best Place to Start is Learning to Putt

I find it interesting that most people begin learning golf by developing a golf swing. Logic tells us that if putting accounts for 40% of your score, it makes better sense to learn putting first. Most players spend less that 10% of their time concentrating on being great putters. If you want to consistently score in the low 80s or upper 70s, I strongly recommend focusing your time on putting first. This will pay big dividends in the long run. You can practice and develop an excellent putting stroke right at home.

The best putting grip I have found over the years is the interlocking grip. This hand position avoids having either hand dominate the putting stroke.

Thus, the hands function as one unit. This is most important in developing a smooth stroke. It took me several months after adopting this change before I transformed my game. This grip helped me feel the putting stroke and the ball at impact. Once I could feel impact, my putting performance began to improve. During this transition, my average number of putts went from 35 to 29 per round.

Thus, I was able to improve my score by six strokes on the greens. What was more interesting, I one putted 28% of the time. Previously, this statistic was 10%. This improvement resulted in more birdies and par saves, thus lowering my overall score.

Secret # 11 - One can make a mistake from the tee box or the fairway. You can make up for the mistake when putting☺.

To improve my putting, I developed the following process:

1) Switched my grip to the interlocking of fingers.

2) I started practicing with my feet close together and positioning the ball in the middle of my stance. This position helped me learn to swing the putter on a pendulum. The back stroke was short and the follow through matched the back swing. My hands were slightly ahead of the ball at address.

3) I tried to stroke the ball with a steady, smooth movement. This was harder than I initially thought since the back stroke with a putter is not long. Striving for a steady, consistent and smooth stroke became the objective. Once I began feeling the putter impact the ball, I knew my putting skills could get better.

4) This is where experiment transitioned into performance. Continuing to use the same set up (feet together, ball in the middle), I began moving my feet apart keeping the ball in the middle of my stance. This helped me identify how far apart to place my feet. After several minutes, I found that having my feet twelve to fourteen inches apart felt the most comfortable.

5) Then, I began adjusting the ball within the stance. Starting with the ball positioned off the left toe, I began rolling putts. By moving the ball position towards the middle of my stance (an inch at a time), I found the ball position where impact would occur each time. This entire process took thirty minutes.

My impact point was about halfway between the center line of my left foot and the middle of my stance. This spot created solid impact each and every time. There was consistency to the stroke and roll of the ball. Once I found this spot, I was able to refine the entire putting stroke.

Secret # 12 - The ball position is affected by the putter design. If the club head is offset, the impact position may vary☺.

Secret # 13 - The lie of the putter can be flat to very upright. Thus, your body's distance from the ball is affected by the equipment☺.

Two major elements are necessary to find a solid and consistent putting stroke: first, no head movement and second, eyes over the ball. The first was hardest to repair. After years of neglecting my putting skills, my eyes would follow the putter head during the stroke at impact. This caused my head to move altering the direction of the ball. It took several weeks to implement better behavior, but I finally became disciplined and my putting skills continued to improve.

The other element (eyes over the ball) was improved with a change in body posture. This too became an experiment. After trying various positions with my head and back, it became clear that my body above the waist was all I needed to adjust. As springtime transitioned into summer, my putting skills became exceptional.

When on the putting green, I try to focus on following a pre-shot routine. (i.e. set the grip, aim the putter head, keep my feet close together, etc.) I position the ball in the middle of my stance, adjust my feet to the desired location, set my posture and finally stroke the ball on the predetermined line.

Another element of being a good putter is the ability to read greens. In short, this means trying to determine the line that the ball needs to roll on to reach the hole. This has become a part of my practice routine. There are two key factors I consider before putting. The first is trying to define the horizontal slope (which way the land slopes left or right).

Secret # 14 - The line of a putt will always be towards the high side of the horizontal slope. The steeper the horizontal slope, the higher the line (break) for the putt☺.

Second, I determine if the putt is uphill or downhill. If a putt is uphill it will require a harder stroke to climb the slope. Conversely, if the putt is downhill a softer stroke is needed, since gravity will increase the speed of the ball.

Secret # 15 - When putting uphill, focus on putting the ball two feet past the hole. When putting downhill, focus on a spot three feet short of the hole☺.

Use this process to identify the line for the putt. First, squat behind the ball to determine the horizontal slope (right to left). Next, stand upright from the same location. Try to imagine drawing a curved line from the ball to the hole. Finally, try to locate spots or marks on the green surface that can help bring the putting line into focus. This will help you see the desired ball tract.

Secret # 16 - Reading the green from both positions will help you avoid misreading the line a majority of the time☺.

Some players spend considerable time trying to read the grain of a green. In layman's terms this means identifying the direction the grass grows. Depending on the region of the country and the type of grass on the greens, some grains are difficult to find. The best place to determine the grain is around the hole.

Secret # 17 -Finding the best line for your putt and making a good stroke will overcome the grain for the most part☺.

There are several key points to remember when putting:

* Look at a putt from two positions: first, squat from behind the ball to find the horizontal slope; second, stand upright in the same location to find the line for the putt.

*On breaking putts...once speed is lost, the grain of the green will turn the ball. Thus, we have two options: you must either putt the ball on a higher line or hit the ball harder. The first option is better. Option two works, but the return putt will be longer.

*Putts inside thirty feet, try to make them unless the horizontal slope is severe or there is a double tier green involved.

*Putts over thirty feet, try to get the ball within two feet of the cup. Occasionally, your first putt will drop in the hole.

*Very seldom will two players see the same line of a putt. Thus, read and stroke the putt on the line you believe is correct.

*If the putt is downhill, putt for a spot three feet short of the hole. The ball will roll out and snuggle up to the hole.

*If the putt is uphill, putt for a spot two feet past the hole. The ball will have enough speed to reach the hole.

Secret # 18 - Focus on the line for the putt, not the hole. Unless you find the line, making putts is largely left to the luck factor☺.

Of all the putters on the market, some of my favorites are the Odyssey series, Ping, Bulls Eye, and the Taylor Made Rosa. All of these putters have great feel and balance. However, if I switch putters, I have to readjust my ball position within my stance and body distance from the ball. Each putter is different.

I recommend that every golfer invest in a quality putter. It is a small price to pay and it will last a lifetime. If you can master the putting game, friendly wagers on Saturday will reimburse you for the putter over time. Also, it will earn you the distinction of being a fine player, which of course is priceless!

C. Chipping
"Getting Up & Down"

The second best place to save strokes is around the green. Oddly enough this part of your game depends on how many greens you hit in regulation. When observing many players over time, amateurs average hitting nine greens per round. Thus, there are nine times that one must chip or pitch during any given round.

The question I encourage all players to ask themselves when getting ready to chip around the green is, "What club do I need to make the shot convert into a putt"? If you minimize the flight time of the ball, two things will occur: first, the shot transitions into a putt very quickly, second, you can read the upcoming putt while the ball is rolling towards or past the hole.

Secret # 19 - Read the horizontal slope of the green and look for the line when chipping just as you do when putting☺.

The sooner the ball begins to roll after chipping, the greater likelihood you can create a one putt situation. This becomes the main strategy of the chipping game.

Secret # 20 - If you try to chip past the hole, you have an opportunity to make the chip shot or read the returning putt☺!

The key to excellent chipping skill is club selection. Club selection depends on four key elements:

1) Distance to the hole,
2) Is the ball resting on an upslope or downslope,
3) How far it is to the green, and
4) Are you chipping into an upslope or a downslope.

Secret # 21 - When chipping on an upslope, take a less lofted club (i.e. lower number on the club). The reason is because the upslope increases the loft of a club causing the ball to have a higher trajectory, thus losing distance☺.

I frequently see amateurs use the same club when chipping. The limited use of club selection works against your objective. The slope of the green and where the ball sits will require one to utilize different clubs most of the time to execute the shot. A majority of the time you will use between a 7 iron and a sand wedge when chipping. Using these five clubs will enable you to create a wide variety of shots to help you save strokes around the green.

Secret # 22 - When the grass is taller than two inches, use a wedge or sand wedge☺.

Below is the routine that I have used to help me enjoy considerable success around the greens.

1) Select a spot where the ball needs to land and start rolling. Remember the closer the ball lands to the hole, the harder it becomes to stop the ball quickly. Thus, the farther you land the ball from the hole, the greater chance you have at reading the upcoming putt.

Secret # 23 -The longer a ball is in the air on a chip shot, the greater backspin required to stop the ball quickly. Thus, controlling the distance a ball rolls is forfeited☺.

2) Position the ball back in your stance, off the right foot. This allows you to impact the ball cleanly, and it also prevents chili dipping. (Chili dipping – the art of advancing the ball six inches)

3) Keep your hands in front of the ball during the shot. This enables you to keep the ball flight low allowing the ball to stay close to the ground. Now the ball can convert to a putt faster.

Have patience when making your club selection for chipping. Practicing a variety of chip shots, (distance to the hole from a variety of lies), around the practice green will help you gain better knowledge and help you become better at club selection. This is where you should experiment with all kinds of lies and club selections. Be imaginative and creative when chipping.

Secret # 24 - If you can get up and down in two strokes half the time, a player can save an average of five strokes per 18 holes☺.

D. Pitching, Fairway Shots, and the Tee Ball

In Chapter A, we reviewed six fundamentals that are keys to building a successful golf game. When practicing, I strongly recommend a player focus on hitting pitch shots between 40 and 80 yards. The reason is because this yardage shot is a mini version of all shots you make from the tee box or in the fairway. The primary difference between the 40 and 80 yard pitch shots and other shots is the length of the back swing.

Think about it, if you can repeat a half swing 100% of the time creating excellent impact, what is to prevent you from repeating that swing with a five iron, a three wood, or a driver? A good golf shot is determined when the club face meets the ball on the downswing.

Secret # 25 – Great golf shots occur within a twelve inch area. The first six inches of the backswing and the first six inches after the club face impacts the ball☺.

Approaching the game with a desire to create solid impact on every shot rather than how far you can hit the ball has benefits. You gain more distance, backspin is increased, scoring improves, the enjoyment factor rises, and the cost factor declines (i.e. lost balls).

Secret # 26 - If you use the same pre-shot routine and address position for all shots, you minimize the number of mistakes created during the round☺.

In putting and chipping, we created a process to reduce strokes during your round. However, your strategy changes from the tee box and when you are in the fairway. Your objective is to avoid making mistakes that increase your score.

From the tee box to the chip shot, your objective should be to keep the ball in the fairway. If you employ the same process for your tee shot, fairway iron, or pitch shot; you will minimize the likelihood of creating a complex game that supports making mistakes. Let's review the aspects of pitching, fairway shots, and the tee ball.

Pitching – That shot between 5 and 75 yards from the green
The hardest shot and least used shot in golf is the pitch shot. It is tough to control the distance of the ball, because there can be so many variables encountered. When I practice, the pitch shot becomes the predominant shot to master. My reason is threefold. First, it becomes the one shot that helps me develop a smooth and consistent swing. Second, I gain considerable feel for controlling the ball's flight. Third, I can work on all of the fundamentals discussed in Chapter A without putting forth considerable effort.

Secret # 27 – If you focus on the one shot you seldom use; you will remove all of the pressure from the game to hit the ball far☺!

This became a major turning point for me. In fact, if I can practice thirty minutes twice a week on this one shot, I can break 80 every weekend. With a good thirty minute warm up and good mental preparation before a round on the weekend, I can stay near 75.

Fairway Shots - That shot between 75 and 220 Yards
A fairway shot is nothing more than a pitch shot with a longer back swing. A majority of the time you can use an iron for your first shot on a Par 3, an iron for your second shot on a Par 4, and an iron for your third shot on a Par 5. Even using a long iron (2, 3, or 4 iron) for the second shot on a Par 5 can be beneficial.

Think about it, if you can develop a repetitive swing with a pitching wedge and let this be your basis for all fairway shots; then you can master hitting all fairway iron shots regardless of where you are on the golf course. In the next three chapters, I'll focus more on how to use irons from the fairway.

Tee Ball - The starting point for each hole

When starting on any hole, ask yourself this question, "Do I need a driver when I tee off on this hole"? Answer honestly! By asking this question on each tee box can save you a lot of strokes. I guarantee that using a driver on every tee box will increase your score in any round. The swing with a driver is very similar to that of a pitch shot. All the fundamentals we discussed earlier (grip, aim, stance, ball position, hand position, and balance) match that of the pitch shot.

Secret # 28 - The driver has a much longer shaft than all other clubs. Thus, the longer shaft requires perfect timing to get the club head square at impact☺.

Since the driver is the hardest club to hit, why not eliminate the club as much as possible from your round? Here are a few guidelines I have developed that may be helpful to you when on the tee box:

On a Par 3 – rarely hit a driver unless the hole is over 240 yards

On a Par 4 under 380 yards:
    * use a 3 metal unless you're into the wind, then a driver
    * if there is trouble left or right, then use a 3 metal
    * downwind and downhill – hit a 2 iron or 4 metal

On a Par 4 greater than 381 yards:
    * you must hit a driver
    * avoid cutting corners and going over hazards

Most of the time on a Par 5, you will tee off with a driver, but consider using a 3 metal at times. A major objective when playing a Par 5 is to preplan the third shot before you take the second shot. If you advance the ball on your second shot to where it lays between 75 to 135 yards from the green, you will leave yourself in a position to create more options for the third shot. Your options can range from a full sand wedge to a three-quarter 8 iron.

When on the tee box or in the fairway, approach all shots with the same focus as a pitch shot: smooth tempo, ¾ swing and emphasize the six fundamentals we outlined in Chapter A:

1) Position the hands on the club and set the grip
2) Aim the club face (positioning the club face behind the ball)
3) Take your stance (keep feet together, ball in the middle)
4) Begin widening your feet and position the ball in the stance
5) Establish your hand position slightly ahead of the ball
6) Finalize your balance

Remember from the tee box or in the fairway to stand behind the ball and visualize the ball's flight path. Utilize targets in the distance (trees, moguls, objects, etc.) to help identify a flight line. Look for a mark in front of the ball on the ground. Aim the club face at the mark using this spot as a guide to the flight line. If you do this, your mental game forgets about distance and swinging hard.

By mastering the pitch shot, it becomes easier to improve hitting fairway shots and the tee ball. You can also feel the impact of the shot faster than if you hit a driver nonstop on the practice tee.

When I applied this process to my own game, my swing fell into a place of tranquility that produced very favorable results. Let your mind focus on a smooth tempo, rather than how far to hit the ball. You will be amazed how the game becomes easier.

Secret # 29 - In golf, finesse will conquer brute force every time☺.

E. Club Selection

A high percentage of the time, players often come up short of the green with their approach shot. There are two reasons for leaving it short of the green:

        1) You "deloft" the club face at impact
        2) You do not select enough club for the shot

1) Delofting can best be described as a condition whereby the club face approaches the ball on the downswing with the toe of the club laying open. In short, the club face slides under the ball. Thus, the ball impacts the club face towards the top edge of the club. This contact point transfers less energy to the ball. A shot will go straight but travels a shorter distance. In Picture A, the club face is square at impact. In Picture B, the club face slides under the ball.

      Picture A   **Picture B**

2) 75% of the time, a golfer will select less club for a shot than needed to reach the target. Players frequently forget to incorporate a multitude of factors when selecting a club.

Wind – wind velocity increases above trees and buildings
Topography – elevation changes may require more or less club
Air temperature – under 50 degrees the ball travels less distance
Pin position – big greens may have a three club variation
Ball position - is the ball (above or below) your feet?

The following example illustrates how these factors affect the club selection process. My 8 iron generally carries 150 yards from a flat lie to a green without an elevation change and no wind. Let's say my ball is resting at the 150 yard marker. The green is 40 yards deep. This makes the front of the green 130 yards and the back of the green 170 yards. There is a gentle rising slope approaching the green, and the green has two levels at the mid-point. The front level is lower than the back. Given a variety of weather conditions, here are the options I may encounter on the shot:

1) Pin on front into a 10 MPH wind   8 iron   130 yds
2) Pin on front with a 20 MPH tail wind   Wedge   130 yds
3) Pin in middle with a cross wind   7 iron   150 yds
4) Pin in back with no wind   5 iron   170 yds
5) Pin on front, 40 degrees, into a wind   7 iron   130 yds

As one can see, my club selection on this shot depends on the elements of nature. To improve your score there must be adjustments, at all times, when shooting into the green. You must also know the distance that you can hit each club from a flat lie to a non-elevated target without wind under normal air temperatures (65 degrees or higher). Below is my personal distance chart from which I start determining club selection:

Driver – 265   3 metal – 230
1 iron – 220 2 iron – 210 3 iron – 200 4 iron – 190 5 iron – 180
6 iron – 170 7 iron – 160 8 iron – 150 9 iron – 140 Wedge – 125
Sand Wedge - 90

Secret # 30 - A player must know their yardage limits when beginning to attack the green. Otherwise, they will give away strokes to par☺.

If I play near the ocean, I deduct 7 yards per club due to being closer to sea level. If I go to the mountains, I add 7 yards per club to adjust for thinner air at higher altitudes. Before playing, check

THE WEATHER CHANNEL for the daily forecast, paying close attention to wind speed and direction.

If you play one course regularly, it is important to know the yardage to the front and back of the green. Also, know whether a green is elevated or downhill from the fairway.

Secret # 31 - When the air temperature falls below 50 degrees, I switch to a lower compression ball; generally, a Lady Titleist. A higher compression ball is harder to compress in cold weather. Thus, it travels less distance☺.

Most golf courses have a flag near the club house. Flags will help you identify the wind's direction and strength.

Secret # 32 – As a ball climbs higher into the air, the wind resistance on the ball may increase or decrease☺.

The reason is because at the surface, wind is restricted by structures and vegetation. Once the ball rises about 30 feet into the air, the wind velocity increases due to the lack of obstructions.

Secret # 33 - Search tree tops to find the direction of the wind☺.

Sometimes you have to guess how much club is needed on a shot. One thing is guaranteed, making no adjustment will produce less than the desired results and it will impact the score card.

F. Course Management or Strategy

Course management or strategy is critical to playing good golf. I believe that golf course architects take a raw piece of land and shape it into a spectacle to be enjoyed. Architects design a hole with a specific plan on how you should approach playing the hole. Here are some suggestions:

1) Using a 3 or 5 metal or a long iron (1, 2, or 3) from the tee box is acceptable. Generally, on a par 4 hole of 380 yards or less, use a 3 metal from the tee box (depending on the wind). The strategy is to position your self for par or better. Short par fours are usually difficult holes. Thus, leaving the driver in the bag can minimize the margin of error.

Secret # 34 - Some of the hardest holes you will play are short par fours ☺.

2) Avoid going over sand traps, hazards or cutting corners. Most architects want you to hit into a landing area (I call this spot the "Happy Place™"). It is easier to make birdies from the "Happy Place™".

In the following illustration, please note the "Happy Place™". The architect wants you to hit your tee ball in the dogleg. Finding this spot with your tee shot is essential to playing better golf.

Secret # 35 - You must know the distance to a "Happy Place™"☺!

3) The shape of the green also affects your approach. If the pin is placed close to the green's perimeter, shoot into the "Happy Place™". This conservative approach will help you save strokes by increasing the number of greens hit in regulation. You will also increase the number of birdie opportunities and record more pars in the process.

In the following illustration, there are three pin placements: A, B, and C. Each pin position creates possible challenges if you aggressively attack the pin. The best strategy is to shoot for the "Happy Place™" and set up a possible birdie and more than likely an easy par.

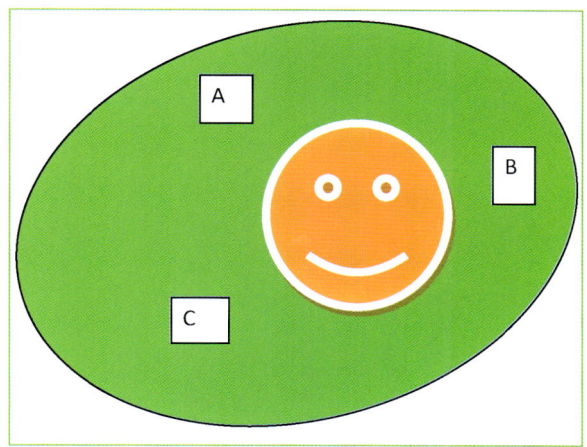

Secret # 36 – The Happy Place™ will help you lower your score☺.

4) Putting strategy……Let's review some key elements from Chapter B:

* Look at a putt from two positions: first, squat from behind the ball to find the horizontal slope; second, stand erect in the same location to find the line.

* On breaking putts…once speed is lost, the grain of the green will turn the ball. Thus, we have two options: you must either putt the ball on a higher line or hit the ball harder. The first option is better. Option two works, but the return putt will be longer.

* Putts inside thirty feet, try to make them unless the horizontal slope is severe or there is a double tier green involved.

* Putts over thirty feet, try to get the ball within two feet of the hole. Occasionally, your first putt will drop in the hole.

* Very seldom will two players see the same line of a putt. Thus, read and stroke the putt on the line you believe is correct.

* If the putt is downhill, putt for a spot three feet short of the hole. The ball will roll out and snuggle up to the hole.

* If the putt is uphill, putt for a spot two feet past the hole. The ball will have enough speed to reach the hole.

* Focus on the line for the putt, not the hole.

The lack of course management or strategy impacts you and the scorecard in many ways:

    1) it increases the time needed to play a round of golf
    2) it increases the need to purchase more golf balls
    3) it contributes to a higher score
    4) it will take away your enjoyment of the day

G. Managing Predicaments

In golf, you rarely find yourself with a perfect lie (i.e. that is where the ball lands on a flat surface). Always search for the little imperfections that will help you make small adjustments to achieve the best possible impact when you swing. Be careful of the slightest downslope, upslope, or side hill lies. These topography variations will surely affect the flight of the ball.

However, there will be times, for whatever reason, you have a mental lapse which produces a very bad shot. You can be assured that when this happens the ball will find a resting place that leaves you in a predicament.

My definition of a predicament is simple, "It is a situation where par is remote. Thus, you must find a way to make bogey!"

When these situations present themselves, your confidence is shaken to the core. Typically, your playing partner(s) will begin to display their "Jay Leno" talents with one-liners or quick wit. How you negotiate a predicament largely depends on one major factor....your attitude! You can manage working through difficult predicaments by creating a positive thought process.

Secret # 37 – Your attitude impacts the scorecard☺!

Earlier, we discussed creating impact by using a consistent ball position in your stance. Getting out of predicaments will require you to modify this approach. Thus, altering the ball's position in your stance is required. Here are four secrets to remember when the ball is on a slope:

Secret # 38 - On a downslope, move the ball towards the right foot and use a more lofted club. Reason - the club arrives at the ball sooner. The shot has a tendency to go right☺.

Secret # 39 - On an upslope, move the ball towards your left foot and you may need a less lofted club. Reason - the club arrives at the ball later. The shot has a tendency to go left☺.

Secret # 40 - When your feet are above the ball, position the ball in the middle of the stance and aim slightly left of your target. The reason is because the club face impacts the ball near the center of your stance. When your feet are above the ball, the ball has a tendency to go right☺.

Secret # 41 - When your feet are below the ball, position the ball in the middle of the stance and aim slightly right of your target. The reason is because the club face impacts the ball near the center of your stance. When your feet are below the ball, the ball has a tendency to go left☺.

When you find yourself in a predicament where the green is surrounded by hazards and sand traps, play for a "Happy Place™" short of the green in the fairway. The objective is to recover from the predicament by advancing the ball to the best possible "Happy Place™". Thus, you position yourself for a chance at par or at the worst, a bogey.

Predicaments occur when you least expect it. Managing the predicament is your best approach. A small percentage of the time, when playing for bogey, you can make par because of a positive attitude. Miracles do happen!

Secret # 42 – Managing a predicament will create self confidence by working through a difficult situation in golf and life☺!

Secret # 43 - Have patience, study the topography and take your time when exiting a predicament☺!!!.

H. Playing from the Sand

Earlier, I commented that avoiding sand traps is part of my strategy. Since I do not get time to practice sand shots, avoiding the sand saves me a lot of strokes.

Sand traps are another form of predicament. There are two different types of sand traps: those found beside or in the fairway and those found around the green. You have to employ a different strategy depending on whether you are in a fairway or green side sand trap. I will discuss each separately.

Fairway Sand Traps

Fairway sand traps add to the beauty of a golf course. However, if you give them little thought when trying to exit the sand trap, it will add strokes to your score card.

Secret # 44 - 85% of the time, when in a fairway sand trap, the lie is not favorable to attack the green. Thus, the strategy is to find a "Happy Place™" in the fairway short of the green☺!

The only time I recommend taking a shot at the green, when in a fairway sand trap, is when the lie is flat and the ball is sitting up (clean lie), as illustrated in the following picture.

In all other predicaments, play for the "Happy Place™". The reason is because exiting the sand trap in one stroke becomes the objective.

Secret # 45 - If the lie in a fairway sand trap is clean, take two clubs more than normal for the yardage. Then, make adjustments for the topography and weather conditions☺!

This secret automatically adjusts for loss of distance that occurs when the club impacts the sand. The best conservative play is to aim for the middle of the green. This will leave room for error if the shot is slightly wayward.

Secret # 46 - When shooting for the green from a fairway sand trap, play the ball from the middle of your stance☺.

Since the shot requires you to pick the ball off the sand, your impact point is slightly altered. There is an exception to this strategy. On the next page, a hole is illustrated to help visualize the risk of shooting for the green from a fairway sand trap. If the ball was positioned at the 125 yard marker, your "Happy Place™" is about 60 to 70 yards from the green. Even if the ball was sitting in a flat spot (clean lie), I seriously doubt if I would attack the green. Too many hazards lay between the ball and the green. Thus, the strategy is to play for a bogey (maybe great par) rather than risk scoring 7 or higher.

54 Secrets To Playing Better Golf

Secret # 47 - If there are hazards (creeks, lakes, out of bounds, etc.) round the green, find a "Happy Place™" in the fairway to advance the ball☺.

Remember, before hitting from a fairway sand trap calculate the yardage to the "Happy Place™"; then select a club.

In Section G – Managing Predicaments, **Secrets 38 through 41** guided you on how to adjust the ball position for slopes and in relationship to your feet. You should use the same thought process when in a fairway sand trap.

Green Side Sand Traps
When in a sand trap around the green, your strategy is to get the ball on the green in one shot. Your goal is to set up a one putt situation but no greater than two putt outcome. To play effectively from a green side sand trap, one must have a good sand wedge. Occasionally, you may need to pitch from the sand. This may occur when you are near the top edge of the sand trap. A wedge or 9 Iron should be most helpful in these predicaments.

When in a green side sand trap, you will make an unusual adjustment in your stance. For the most part, you aim your feet left of the target and open the club face.

Club face is square to the ball   **Club face is open to the ball**

Opening the club face allows the club to slide under the ball, lifting the ball from the sand. The most difficult part when playing from a green side sand trap is that you must hit one inch behind the ball. This shot takes a lot of practice.

Secret # 48 - To open the club face; rotate the club to the right, not your hands☺!

For the most part, green side sand traps are smaller and contain severe slopes. Thus, you must adjust the ball position in your stance to adjust for the slopes. (Refer to **Secrets 38 to 41**).

Earlier, I discussed finding a "Happy Place™" when exiting fairway sand traps. The same applies with a green side sand trap. Always look for two "Happy Places" on the green before exiting the green side sand trap.

Secret # 49 - The "Happy Place™" will be those areas on the green where the surface is relatively flat☺!

The most important part of playing from a green side sand trap is to remember you do not need a large, hard swing to advance the ball.

Secret # 50 - A majority of the time a swing comparable to a chip or pitch shot is all that is needed to advance the ball on the green☺!

The sand shot requires considerable touch (finesse) and practice. Typically most sand traps have a multitude of slopes making it very hard to exit with great precision. Thus, avoiding sand traps helps lower your score.

Here are a few rules to remember when exiting a green side sand trap:

    1) Do not let the club touch the ground.
    2) Wiggle your feet until sand covers the sole of your shoes
    3) Use a chip or pitch shot when exiting a green side sand trap
    4) Exiting a sand trap in one stoke is the objective
    5) Always look for two "Happy Places™"
    6) Always rake the sand trap after completing your shot.

Secret # 51 - 99% of the time you will use a sand wedge, hit one inch behind the ball and always open the club face☺.

I. The Mental Side of Golf

Ninety percent of golf is a mental game. It is hard to imagine with all the intricate details of the game that this would be possible. When I watch professionals, whether it be ladies or men, there is a stare that a player gets prior to the shot. Notice their eyes. They are focused, almost transfixed, on the upcoming shot. As a player, it is a great feeling. You know you're in control. Your mind is operating at the speed of an Intel processor: calculating yardage, checking the wind direction, reviewing the topography, then selecting a club, and feeling the tempo needed to make the shot. You review all the variables in less than a minute; and when you're playing in front of a gallery, no one else exists. It's just you, the ball, a club, and nature.

Then it happens, in less than two seconds, you swing and the club strikes the ball, and you know at the moment of impact that it was a great shot. Oh my, what a feeling!

Secret #52 – The mental game begins as you approach your next shot whether you are walking or riding in a cart☺.

Before making a shot take a few seconds to clear your head and focus your thoughts on the shot. It is similar to when you're at work. At the office you focus on a project or any given task at hand. It is the same in golf. Just pay attention. Focus on all the natural elements around you.

Secret #53 – Allow ninety seconds of time to pre-plan and execute a shot. Focus your energy on calculating yardage, checking the wind, elevation changes, and most importantly, the ball position in relationship to the topography☺!

Implementing this secret will reduce strokes and reinforce your confidence tremendously.

On average it takes about four and one half hours to play 18 holes. If your average score is 80 and you take ninety seconds to pre-plan and execute your shots; you will use two hours of the time playing golf. The other two and one half hours can be spent enjoying friends, taking in nature or smelling the azaleas. Between shots, enjoy your company and surroundings. When it's time to hit the ball, focus for ninety seconds.

J. Course Etiquette

Golf has always been considered a gentleman's game. It is a game where your behavior speaks volumes about your character. Golf is also a game to be enjoyed by your self or with others. It provides relaxation, fresh air, and exercise. Above all, golf creates a chance for you to socialize with friends or complete strangers.

Below are tips for course etiquette. These tips will enhance your character, reward you with respect, and others will want to play golf with you!

1) If you use colorful language, keep your voice very low around the club house, parking lot, women, children, and microphones
2) Dress appropriately when playing golf
3) Always check in with the pro shop before playing
4) If you play a fivesome, get permission from the pro shop first
5) If there is a starter, check in with them before your tee time
6) Start from the first or tenth tee
7) Observe the rules of the day, especially during the rainy season
8) Stay on the cart path means stay on the cart path
9) Observe cart directional signs
10) When in a cart, use the 90 degree rule to exit the cart path
11) Keep pull carts off tee boxes, greens, and out of sand traps
12) Remember, foursomes have the right of way on a golf course
13) Place your bag on the same side of the cart where you sit
14) Practice or warm up in designated areas
15) Do not use the course as your private practice area
16) When using a golf cart, avoid squealing the tires
17) Stay in the cart until it comes to a full stop
18) Before moving a golf cart, check for other players in the area
19) Be quiet and stand still when another player is making a shot
20) Play between and behind the tee markers
21) If available, put sand in a divot on the tee box or replace a divot
22) If you find a golf club or head cover, turn it into the pro shop

23) Help a player find his tee
24) Watch a player's ball after each shot and help them locate it
25) Offer to help a player find a lost ball
26) Replace a divot in the fairway
27) Stay positive, regardless of your predicament
28) Enter a sand trap from the low side
29) Always rake a sand trap after making a shot
30) Leave the rake outside of a sand trap
31) Repair your ball mark on every green
32) Mark your ball on the green with a coin before lifting it
33) Don't walk in a player's line when on the green
34) After removing a flag stick from the hole, lay it off the green
35) Avoid throwing the flag stick down
36) If you hole out first, take control of the flag stick
37) Avoid using anything but a putter when on the green
38) Pick up a partner's club when exiting the green
39) The one with the best score, tees off first on the next hole
40) Always congratulate a player for achievement
41) Shake your playing partner's hand after completing play
42) When losing a match, be gracious
43) When winning a match or tournament, be humble
44) Count all your strokes after a hole
45) Always check your score card and sign it before turning it in
46) If you have a caddy, listen to them for suggestions
47) Tip your caddy 20%
48) Never blame your caddy for a bad shot
49) Let faster players through on a tee box
50) Always tip your pro after a lesson
51) Pick up trash blowing around the golf course
52) Remove all trash from your cart after play and put in a trash can
53) Learn the rules of golf
54) Be sure to thank the pro shop before leaving the course

Secret #54 - How you behave and act on the golf course will define your reputation and character. Your behavior can open and close doors to the future☺!

K. Tracking Your Performance
"Keep It Simple"

In any endeavor, it is important to measure your progress towards achieving your goals. In golf, my major objective is to create the best possible impact on each stroke. The feedback for this objective occurs immediately upon striking the ball. Thus, it is not recorded on the score card but becomes a private observation.

However, in golf, as in any other game, you keep score so that you and others may judge your performance. The total score reflects the overall outcome of the day. The statistics I pay close attention to are those that help me measure my performance long term. Below are the performance measures that I have found beneficial:

* Date of the round
* Name of golf course
* Par for 9 or 18 holes
* Score – only record those scores for 9 or 18 holes
* Fairways hit – goal is to get 80% of your drives in the fairway
* Up & Down – goal is to get up and down 50% of the time in two
* Greens in regulation – goal is to average 12 GIRs per round
* Putts per round – goal is to have less than 30 putts
* Number of 1 putts – goal is to have 5 one putts per round
* Balls lost – goal is not to lose a ball
* Sand strokes – goal is to get out of the sand trap in one shot
* Penalty shots – goal is to have none

When I look at a score card and find a double bogey or worse, I know that my mental game was absent. Thus, my thoughts were on something other then golf for a brief moment.

L. **Golf Terminology**

If by chance a person who has not played golf purchases this book, it is appropriate to include a section about golf terminology. I hope these definitions are easy to understand. If you have any questions, please e-mail me at rgm@golf54secrets.com.

 This symbol is known as my "Happy Place™". It is the imaginary target I aim for when playing golf.

Ace – making a shot in one stroke from the tee box to the hole
Address – occurs when you position the club head behind the ball
Attack the flag – this is when you shoot straight for the flag stick
Ball mark – the indentation made on the green by a ball
Ball position – this is where the ball rests between the feet
Ball washer – a device found at each tee box to clean your ball
Birdie – taking one less stroke than par
Bogey – taking one more stroke than par
Break – when the ball turns left or right on a green
Bunker – a depression in the earth that has grass rather than sand
Chili dipping – the art of advancing a ball six inches in one stroke
Chipping – a short stroke advancing the ball a short distance
Club head - the end of the club used for hitting the ball
Conceding a putt – giving your playing partner the remaining putt
Cup – the plastic item found in the hole which holds the flag stick.
Deloft – when the club face slides under the ball
Divot – a chunk of turf extracted from the earth
Dogleg – this is a bend or turn in the fairway
Double bogey – taking two more strokes than par
Double eagle – taking 3 fewer strokes than par (applies to par 5s)
Driver – a number one metal generally used on the tee box
Eagle – taking two strokes less than par
Fade – when a shot proceeds straight, then drifts to the right
Fairway – the mowed area separating the tee box and the green
Fairway metals – oversized or large headed clubs
Flag stick – pole with a flag to help you find the hole
Fore – what to yell when an errant shot approaches a player

Fringe – the short grassy area circling the green (a.k.a. frog-hair)
Gimme – picking up your ball when it rests close to the hole
Green – the area of smooth short turf surrounding the flag stick
Green in regulation – reaching a green in the allotted strokes
Grain – the direction grass grows anywhere on the golf course
Grip – the end of the golf club you hold onto with your hands
Handicap – the average number of strokes over par for 18 holes
Hole in One – sinking the ball in the hole with one shot from the tee
Hole out – when a player hits the ball in a hole from off the green
Hook – when the ball turns to the left very quickly after a shot
Horizontal slope – the left to right slope of the terrain
Hosel – the space where the shaft and club head connect
Impact – that is when the club face strikes the ball
Landing area – the "Happy Place™"
Lateral hazard – bad stuff to the left or right of a fairway
Line – the path a ball takes as it rolls towards the hole on a green
Lob wedge – similar to a sand wedge with a higher degree of loft
Loft – the angle or tilt on the club face
Long irons – 2, 3, or 4 irons
Luck – a byproduct of hard work
Middle irons – 5, 6, or 7 irons
Mogul – small hump on the surface of the ground
Mulligan – a free second shot on the first tee
One putt – when you stroke your first putt and it goes in the hole
Out of Bounds – the outer perimeter of the golf course
Par – taking the scheduled number of strokes on a hole
Penalty shot – extra stroke incurred when a ball goes wayward
Pin – another term for flag stick
Pitch or pitching – advancing the ball between 5 and 75 yards
Predicament - a situation where par is remote.
Putting – a light stroke made on the green
Quadruple bogey – taking four more strokes than par
Round – playing 18 holes of golf
Rough – that area of taller grass bordering the fairway or green
Sand trap – depressions in the earth containing sand
Sand wedge – a very lofted club used to exit a sand trap

Scoring lines – the indentations across the club face
Shaft - the tube between the grip and the hosel
Short irons – 8, 9, or Wedge
Slice – when the ball turns to the right very quickly after a shot
Snowman – taking an 8 on any hole
Soft spikes – the items attached to the soles of your shoe
Stroke and Distance – when a ball goes out of bounds, in the water, or is lost; a player must replay the shot from the original spot. Thus, forfeiting the distance gained and add one stroke.
Tee – a small peg on which the ball is placed on the tee
Tee box – the starting point of each hole
Tee markers – two objects found on a tee box
Triple bogey – taking three more strokes than par
Up & Down – when you chip up on the green and one putt
Water hazard – generally a pond, lake, or creek

54 Secrets To Playing Better Golf Progress Chart

Date	Golf Course	Par	Score	Fairways Hit	Up & Down	Greens in Reg	Putts per Round	Number 1 putts	Balls Lost	Sand Strokes	Penalty Strokes
4-Jan	Chestnut	36	40	7 of 9	2 of 2	7	15	4	2	2	1 Sample

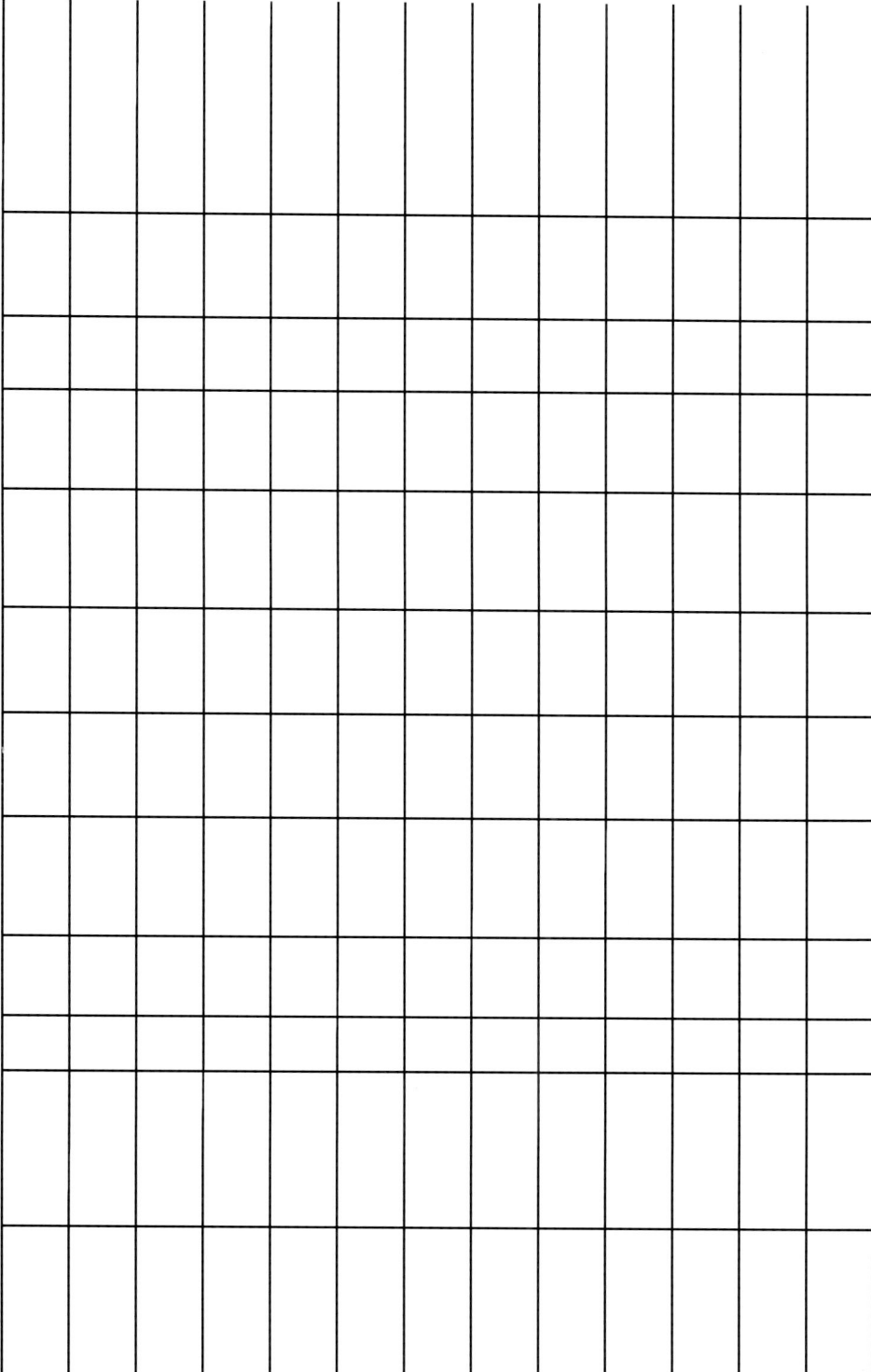